# A New True Book

# AIR POLLUTION

### By Darlene R. Stille

### CHILDRENS PRESS ®

### CHICAGO

**Dangerous chemicals in smoke pollute the air.**

PHOTO CREDITS

Art—Tom Dunnington, 8 (left)

© Cameramann International, Ltd.—6 (left), 23 (top right), 32 (left), 38 (right), 40, 44 (right)

The Marilyn Gartman Agency—© Lee Balterman, 16; © Everett C. Johnson, 21 (right)

Illustrations—Reprinted with permission of *The New Book of Knowledge*, 1989 edition, © Grolier Inc., 12

© Norma Morrison—29 (left), 32 (right), 42 (2 photos), 45 (right)

North Wind Picture Archives—25 (2 photos)

Photri—Cover, 4, 6 (right), 8 (right), 10 (left), 19 (2 photos), 26 (right), 44 (left)

Root Resources—© Grace Lanctot, 14 (top); © Don & Pat Valenti, 31 (right); © Richard Young, 38 (left)

Shostal Associates/SuperStock International, Inc.—2, 10 (right), 17 (right), 26 (left), 34 (left); © Eric G. Carle, 17 (left); © Wm. Thompson, 34 (right)

Tom Stack & Associates—© Tom Stack, 5 (top right); © Gary Milburn, 14 (bottom left); © Jack Swenson, 21 (left); © W. Perry Conway, 23 (bottom right); © John Shaw, 31 (left); © T. Kitchin, 45 (left); © Rad Planck, 45 (center)

Third Coast Stock Source—© Jack Kurtz, 29 (right)

Valan—© M. Julien, 5 (left); © Kennon Cooke, 5 (bottom right), 23 (left); © Y.R. Tymstra, 14 (bottom right); © Dr. A. Farquhar, 18 (left); © Chris Malazdrewicz, 18 (right), © A.B. Joyce, 36

Cover: Smog, Mexico City

Library of Congress Cataloging-in-Publication Data

Stille, Darlene R.
  Air pollution / by Darlene R. Stille.
    p.    cm. — (A New true book)
  Includes index.
  Summary: Discusses the benefits of air, its pollution, and the harmful effects of and ways of avoiding air pollution.
    ISBN 0-516-01181-2
    1.  Air—Pollution—Economic aspects—Juvenile literature. [1.  Air—Pollution.  2.  Pollution.]
I.  Title.
HC79.A4S75   1990                         89-25348
363.73'92—dc20                            CIP
                                          AC

# TABLE OF CONTENTS

# AIR IS ALL AROUND US

We cannot see clean air.
But air is all around us.
We can feel air. The
wind is air that is moving.

We can see what
happens when the wind
blows and air moves. A
gentle wind rustles leaves.
A strong wind makes trees
sway back and forth. Moving
air can be very powerful.
Even though we cannot

5

Polluted air can often be seen as a gray or brownish
haze hanging close to the ground like fog.

see clean air, the movement
of air tells us that it is
all around us.

Sometimes we can see
polluted air. Polluted air is
dirty air.

# AIR IS ALL AROUND THE EARTH

Air surrounds the earth like a big blanket. This blanket of air is called the atmosphere.

The atmosphere goes up for about 50 miles above the earth. Beyond this, the air gets thinner and thinner and gradually trails off into outer space.

The atmosphere makes all life on earth possible. It holds in the warmth from

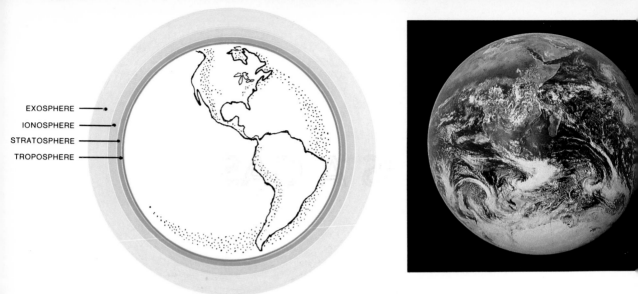

EXOSPHERE
IONOSPHERE
STRATOSPHERE
TROPOSPHERE

Each of the four layers of the atmosphere (left) has a different air temperature. This view of the earth from space (right) shows swirling white clouds in the atmosphere.

the sun. It blocks out harmful rays from the sun. Plants and animals need air to live.

Air pollution can rise up into the atmosphere. The winds carry polluted air for many miles. Polluted air can damage the atmosphere.

# AIR IS A GAS

Air is not liquid like water. Air is not solid like wood. Air is a gas.

Gases go everywhere unless they are held in by something. That is why air is all around us. That is why when air goes up higher and higher above the earth it gets thinner and thinner.

We can capture air.
When we blow up a
balloon, we are capturing
air. The more air we blow
into the balloon, the bigger
it gets. If we blow in more

10

air than it can hold, the balloon will burst.

Air is a mixture of invisible gases. A gas called nitrogen makes up most of the air. The second most plentiful gas in air is called oxygen. Air also contains small amounts of other gases, such as carbon dioxide and ozone.

# AIR MAKES LIFE POSSIBLE

We cannot live without air. We breathe air through our noses and into our lungs. In our lungs, oxygen from the air enters our blood and is carried to every cell in our bodies.

Human beings need to breathe clean air in order to be healthy.

**THE RESPIRATORY SYSTEM**

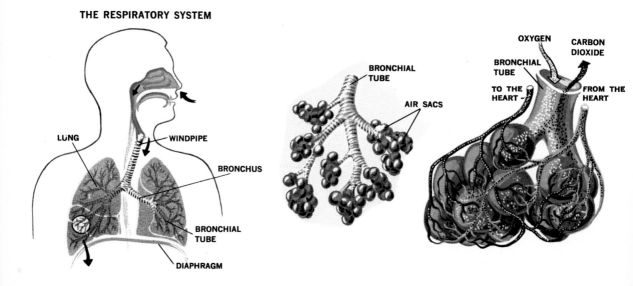

We need oxygen to help
our bodies use food for
energy.

When we breathe out,
we exhale carbon dioxide.
All animals take in oxygen
and give off carbon dioxide.

All plants take in carbon
dioxide and give off oxygen.
Plants use carbon dioxide
and sunlight to make their
food. By taking in carbon
dioxide and giving off
oxygen, plants help keep
the proper balance of
gases in the air.

Steam and smoke from factories and refineries
may carry dirt and poisonous gases into the air.

# WHAT POLLUTES AIR?

Many activities of human beings pollute air. People pollute air by allowing chemicals, poisonous gases, and tiny particles of dirt to get into the air.

Factories and power plants that burn coal pollute air by giving off smoke. The smoke contains dirty particles and gases that do not belong in air. This pollution gets into the air when smoke goes out through smokestacks.

Fumes that come out of automobile tail pipes pollute the air.

Automobiles pollute the air by giving off exhaust fumes. The fumes are created when gasoline is burned in the car's engine. The gasoline does not burn up completely, and the unburned chemicals come out of the tail pipe as

If lead is added to gasoline, tiny lead particles are released in automobile exhaust fumes. These lead particles enter the air we breathe and settle on the soil.

gases and pollute the air.

Another pollutant in gasoline is lead. Lead is sometimes added to gasoline to help engines run more smoothly. At one time, all gasoline contained lead. But unleaded gasoline is now more popular.

17

Smoke from a wood stove (left) and dried-out soil
carried by the wind in a dust storm (right)

Heating systems also pollute the air. Smoke from the chimneys in houses contains chemical fumes. These fumes come from burning oil, gas, coal, or wood.

Nature also causes air pollution. After a long dry spell, winds blow dust particles into the air.

Gas and dust from erupting volcanoes pollute the air.

Volcanoes that erupt
may also cause air
pollution. Gas and dust
from the eruption are
blown into the air.
Sometimes the gas and
dust rise high into the
atmosphere and are
carried for great distances. **19**

# WHERE POLLUTED AIR IS FOUND

Air pollution caused by people is found mainly in and around cities. In cities, there are many cars on streets and highways. The exhaust fumes from the cars go into the air.

Sunlight causes a chemical reaction in the exhaust fumes that creates a type of pollution called smog. The word *smog*

Automobile exhaust fumes and smoke from factories are the main causes of smog in cities.

comes from two other words— *smoke* and *fog*.

Around cities, there are many factories. The smoke from factories and power plants goes into the air. The more factories there are, the more air pollution they cause. Dirt particles in smoke from factories cling to droplets of water in the air and create another type of smog.

In cities, there are many houses, stores, and other buildings. In winter, their chimneys give off smoke from burning oil, gas, coal, and wood.

Because all these sources of pollution are close together, air pollution is worse in cities.

Cities such as Montreal, Canada (left), Los Angeles (top right), and Denver (bottom right) have special smog problems because the surrounding mountains keep the wind from blowing pollution away.

Weather conditions may also make smog worse. If warm air in the atmosphere moves in over cool air near the ground, these layers of air trap the pollution.

23

# POLLUTION AROUND THE WORLD

Air pollution occurs all over the world. It first became a problem more than 100 years ago in England, when coal-burning factories were built.

Pollution then became a problem in the United States, especially in areas where steel mills and oil refineries were built, such as Pittsburgh, Pennsylvania, and Gary, Indiana.

In the 1800s, factories in Sheffield, England, and Pittsburgh, Pennsylvania, caused air pollution.

Factories in Europe also created air pollution, especially along the Rhine River in Germany.

One of the countries with the worst air pollution today is China. In China, factories burn a type of coal that causes very bad pollution.

Small-scale steel production (above) contributes to air pollution in China. Children in Japan (right) wear masks on days when pollution levels are high.

This coal is cheap, and the Chinese need it to develop their country. But it creates thick smog that makes breathing difficult. In Chinese cities, the people often wear masks to protect their noses, throats, and lungs from this pollution.

In the United States today, pollution from car exhaust fumes is a major problem. The smog that is created by this type of pollution is especially bad in cities in the West and Southwest. Because there are not many buses or trains in these cities, most people use their cars to move around.

Los Angeles, California, and Phoenix, Arizona, are two cities with a serious smog problem.

# AIR POLLUTION IS HARMFUL

Polluted air is harmful to people. It can even cause sickness.

The main pollutant in smog made by the chemical reaction of car exhaust fumes and sunlight is a gas called ozone. Ozone is related to oxygen. But ozone is harmful to people. It makes the eyes water and irritates the linings of the nose, throat, and lungs.

Smog in Tokyo, Japan (left), and in Chicago, Illinois (right)

The ozone in smog can make older people, babies, and people with lung diseases very sick. It can even cause death. On days when smog is very bad, people who could be harmed by smog are told to stay indoors.

Lead fumes from leaded gasoline can cause lead poisoning. It harms the blood, brain, and liver.

Chemical pollutants from factories can cause serious lung diseases, including lung cancer.

Chemicals in smoke from factories and power plants rise into the atmosphere, mix with water droplets, and form acid rain. This rain falls many miles away from the factories and power plants.

Left: When acid rain soaks into the ground, the chemical balance
of soil is changed and trees die. Right: Stone buildings
and statues can be eaten away by the chemicals in acid rain.

Acid rain kills fish in
lakes. It kills trees and
other plants. It even
damages the paint on cars
and wears away stone. **31**

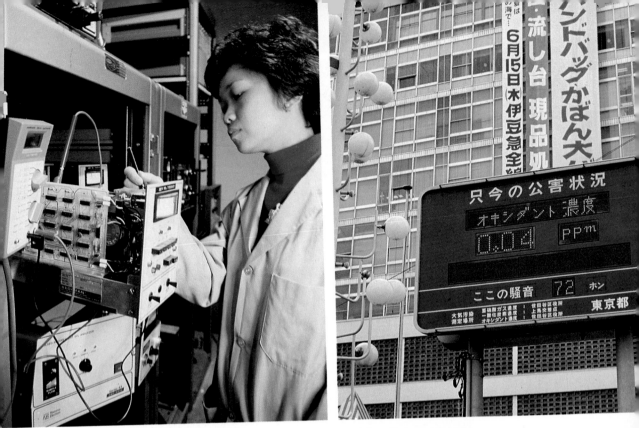

Left: A technician checks equipment used to test for the presence of the gas carbon monoxide, a dangerous air pollutant. Right: A sign on a street in Tokyo gives readings for pollutants.

Other chemicals from factories can also wear away the stone in statues and on buildings. These pollutants also make metals wear away faster.

# INDOOR AIR POLLUTION

Air pollution is also found indoors. Indoor and outdoor air pollution are caused by very different things.

Indoor air pollution can be caused by smoke from a fireplace, fumes from paint, glue, felt-tip markers, hair sprays, and insect sprays.

One of the worst indoor air pollutants is tobacco smoke. Someone who

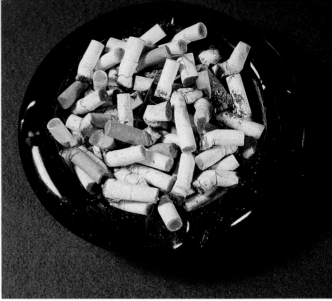

The many chemicals found in tobacco smoke are a source of indoor air pollution, especially in poorly ventilated rooms.

smokes cigarettes, cigars, or a pipe blows smoke into the air. The smoke in the air is inhaled by everyone, even those who do not smoke.

These pollutants can

make you sick. They can give you a headache or an upset stomach. They can make you dizzy or short of breath. Sometimes they can even lead to cancer.

Another major indoor air pollutant is a gas called radon. Radon escapes from soil, stones, bricks, and sometimes from water.

Radon gives off radiation that can be harmful. Radon can cause lung diseases, including cancer.

Insulating this attic will help save on energy because less fuel will be used to keep the inside air warm.

Indoor air pollution became a problem after houses were made more airtight to hold in heat.

But airtight houses and buildings also keep in smoke, fumes, radon gas, and other air pollutants. Because of this, the air inside many houses is more polluted than the most-polluted outdoor air.

# WHAT TO DO ABOUT AIR POLLUTION

There are ways to get rid of air pollution. Outdoor air pollution and indoor air pollution are treated in different ways.

Outdoor air pollution can be controlled by preventing chemicals, poisonous gases, and dirt particles from getting into the atmosphere.

Cars cause less pollution now than they once did

Left: A cutaway view of a catalytic converter. Right: An automobile being tested for acceptable levels of pollutants in its exhaust.

because exhaust fumes are controlled today. Most cars now use lead-free gasoline. They also have devices called catalyic converters that remove the poisonous gases from exhaust fumes. Automobile makers today are trying to

develop engines that burn
almost all the gasoline
that goes into them.

Smokestacks on many
factories and power plants
are now equipped with
devices that remove
chemicals, dirt particles,
and poisonous gases from
the smoke before it goes
out of the smokestack.

Factories must also
control the fumes from
the chemicals used to
manufacture products.

The devices on the roof of this electric power plant control pollution.

They cannot allow certain chemicals to escape into the air.

Indoor air pollution can be controlled by allowing outside air to come inside. The simplest way to do this is by just opening a window. Fans also help to circulate air.

But opening a window can be a problem during cold weather, because heat also escapes from the house. To conserve heat and also cut down on indoor air pollution, special air-moving systems can be built into houses.

Small electric air filters clean the indoor air by removing tobacco smoke and smoke from fireplaces. Vents over gas stoves will remove gas fumes.

Plants help refresh indoor air
by taking in carbon dioxide
and giving off oxygen.

House plants also
absorb air pollutants. So
not only are plants pretty,
they are also good for
your health!

Kits are made to test
buildings for radon. The
kits are set out indoors
for a few days, and then
sent to a laboratory to be
analyzed. If the test shows
high radon levels, several
things can be done.
Cracks in basement floors
and walls can be sealed
to keep the radon gas

outside. Filters can be put on water pipes to remove radon. Special paint can be put on walls to keep the radon from entering the building.

Air pollution is a serious problem and it harms people, animals, plants,

Left: A monkey deformed by pollution in Japan. Below: The city of Los Angeles under a heavy cover of smog.

and even buildings. But air
pollution can be controlled.
The people of the world
must work together to keep
our air clean.

# WORDS YOU SHOULD KNOW

**acid rain**(ACIHD RAYN)—rainwater that has a high acid content because of pollutants

**airtight**(ayr • TITE)—sealed so that air cannot get in or out

**analyze**(AN • uh • lyze)—to break a material down into its parts and to identify the parts

**atmosphere**(AT • muss • fear)—the blanket of air that surrounds the earth

**carbon dioxide**(KAR • bin dye • OX • ide)—a gas that is present in the air in small amounts

**catalytic converter**(kat • uh • LIH • tik kun • VER • ter)—a device that converts automobile exhaust fumes into mostly harmless products

**chemical reaction**(KEM • ih • kil re • ACK • shun)—the rearrangement of atoms or parts of atoms in substances to form different substances

**chemicals**(KEM • ih • kilz)—materials used in many manufacturing processes; chemicals are often harmful to living things

**erupt**(ih • RUHPT)—to burst out, as melted rock, gases, and dust from a volcano

**exhaust fumes**(egs • AWST FYOOMZ)—the gases from partially burned fuel given off by an engine

**filter**(FIHL • ter)—a device that cleans air by trapping harmful particles as the air passes through it

**gas**(GASS)—a substance that is not solid or liquid, but flows freely and is able to expand indefinitely

**lead**(LEHD)—a heavy metal found in some gasolines; lead can be harmful to people

**nitrogen**(NY • truh • jin)—a gas in the air

**oxygen**(AHX • ih • jin)—a gas found in the air; humans and animals need oxygen to breathe

**ozone**(OH • zohn)—a special form of oxygen that is harmful to
  people
**particles**(PAR • tih • kilz)—very tiny bits of matter
**pollution**(puh • LOO • shun)—the dirtying of the earth's air, water,
  and land
**radon**(RAY • dahn)—a radioactive gas found in the soil
**refineries**(rih • FYNE • er • eez)—places where crude oil is made
  into gasoline and other fuels
**smog**(SMAWG)—a polluted haze formed when sunlight acts on
  the fumes put into the air by automobile exhausts

# INDEX

**About the Author**

*Darlene R. Stille is a Chicago-based science writer and editor.*